JN115458

Aikido nyumon : seikaku ~~~ *Kiwameru*
by Mitsuteru,Ueshiba, was published in Japanese,
©Naigai Publishing Co.LTD, 2019.

Translation copyright ©2020 by Naigai Publishing Co.LTD

Naigai Publishing Co.LTD

2-1-11 Higashiueno
 Taito-ku Tokyo, Japan 110-8578
Telephone + 81-3-5830-0368
Facsimile + 81-3-5830-0378
https://www.naigai-p.co.jp
ISBN 978-4-86257-513-5
Printed in Japan

Contents

Demonstrated by Mitsuteru Ueshiba, Director of the Hombu Dojo of Aikido
Demonstrated (as *uke*) by Terumasa Hino, Instructor at the Hombu Dojo of Aikido
                          and Akira Matsumura, Instructor at the Hombu Dojo of Aikido
Translated by Yoshifumi Saito
Photography by Sonobe Yasuo Photographing Office LLC
Book Design by Akihiro Goto

Preface

In aikido, you cope with your opponent's attack in its peculiar movements, slide into his or her dead spot to apply a throwing or holding technique. Its techniques are so structured that you exert your physical power smoothly in a combination of natural movements that agree with the law of nature.

In a training session, trainees observe their instructor's demonstration of techniques, pair up with their partners, and practice them on each other as *uke* (on whom techniques are applied) and *tori* (who copes with attacks and applies techniques) alternately. They keep practicing their right and left variations of techniques in a well-balanced way and train themselves mentally as well as physically.

One of the chief purposes of aikido is to elevate each other technically and mentally through training. Aikido has no contest because it disapproves of competition. Instead, it encourages trainees to respect each other and work with each other in harmony.

In aikido training, trainees keep practicing techniques, depending on their skills and experiences, for the purpose of developing their mind and body, and therefore anybody can practice the art. Daily training is good for your health, of course, but it also naturally makes you positive and confident in handling anything you come across in your everyday lives. Dojo, where varieties of people get together regardless of age, sex, profession, and nationality, will greatly help you understand human relationships.

The quickest way to develop your aikido skills is to 'master the basics properly'. In aikido training, you first learn positioning, bodily movements such as *irimi* and *tenkan*, and breathing methods (*kokyu-ho*) for developing *kokyu-ryoku*. Basic bodily movements constitute the basis of all the techniques of aikido. Mastering basic movements, therefore, is the very first step you need to take to go on to the next stage. Without mastering them properly you cannot expect to develop your skills.

The reader of this book, I guess, is someone who is interested in learning aikido or who has just started learning it. I would strongly advise you to listen with respect to what your instructor says at dojo and try to understand, without any preconceived idea, what each movement means.

This book has a greater number of sequence photographs than other books on aikido techniques previously published. This will help beginners to understand what they need to pay attention in mastering basic movements. It also has many close-up photographs and photographs taken from some different angles, which I hope will make techniques more understandable. It will also be of great help to instructors in charge of beginners and children.

The basics explained in this book constitute the fundamentals of aikido techniques. Therefore you have to keep practicing them even after you are promoted to higher ranks. I hope this book will help you to check what you have learned by observing your instructor's demonstrations at your dojo and thereby improve your skills.

You can master the basics solely by repeated training. You may sometimes feel training painful. However, if you keep practicing aikido, you will find the result rewarding. The repetition of everyday training is sure to bring about your technical as well as mental development.

Kisshomaru Ueshiba, my grandfather and the second Doshu, never failed to take charge of morning sessions as long as he was in Tokyo. Moriteru Ueshiba, my father and the incumbent Doshu, has followed his father's example, and I am now following the example.

The point is to keep practicing naturally with the basics in mind. I also hope that you keep training, always desiring to improve yourself.

Mitsuteru Ueshiba

Director of the Hombu Dojo of Aikido

Before You Start Training

Bowing

When you practice aikido, you bow with respect to the training hall, your instructor, and your fellow trainees. By bowing you make sure of how ready you are for training. Bowing to each other also helps you and your training partner to compose yourselves and thereby prevent injuries.

❶ You sit face to face with your training partner with a proper space in between.

❷ You and your partner put their both hands on the mat and bow to each other. You need to take care that you should not stiffen your neck or bend your back. You sit up straight again.

Hidari-hanmi   *Migi-hanmi*

Foot position when you take a *hanmi* stance

Kamae

In aikido training, you take a *hanmi* stance to face your training partner. You put your left foot forward to take a *hidari-hanmi* stance, right foot to take a *migi-hanmi* stance.

Hidari-ai-hanmi   *Migi-ai-hanmi*

Hidari-gyaku-hanmi   *Migi-gyaku-hanmi*

You always take a *hanmi* stance to each other. However, the type of the *hanmi* stance you take depends on the technique you practice.

In aikido, we use the word *tori* to refer to one of the training pair who applies techniques and the word *uke* to the other on whom they are applied. When both of the pair, *tori* and *uke*, take the same *hanmi* stance, they are described as taking an *ai-hanmi* stance to each other. When they take mutually different left-right variations of *hanmi* stance, they are described as taking a *gyaku-hanmi* stance to each other. *Ai-hanmi* can be further subdivided into *hidari-ai-hanmi* (when *tori* takes a *hidari-hanmi* stance) and *migi-ai-hanmi* (when *tori* takes a *migi-hanmi* stance), *gyaku-hanmi* into *hidari-gyaku-hanmi* (when *tori* takes a *hidari-hanmi* stance) and *migi-gyaku-hanmi* (when *tori* takes a *migi- hanmi* stance).

How to Stand Up

❶ Sit in the formal *seiza* posture.
❷ Take the *kiza* posture by sitting on tiptoes.
❸ Bring one of your knees slightly backward.

How to Sit Down

❶ Stand straight.
❷ Bring one of your feet slightly backward.
❸ Lower yourself, keeping your posture straight, and put the back knee onto the mat.

❹ Raise the other knee.
❺ Stand up in the position.
❻ Draw the back foot up to the other and stand straight.

❹ Put the other knee onto the mat as well.
❺ Sit on tiptoes, put your knees together, and change your sitting posture
om *kiza* to *seiza*.

Front

Back

Important Points to Remember When You Stand Up

❶~❷ Before you stand up from the *seiza* posture, you first sit on your tiptoes in the *kiza* posture. You need consciously keep your posture straight when standing up.

Shikko

Shikko is a method of walking that you need to use in applying sitting techniques.

❶ Sit in the *seiza* posture.
❷ Take the *kiza* posture by sitting on tiptoes.
❸ Twist your body clockwise, raising your left knee forward, and draw your right foot up to your hips.
❹~❺ Put your left knee down onto the mat, twist your body anticlockwise, raising your right knee forward, and draw your left foot up to your hips.
❻~❽ Repeat these movements.
❾ Sit in the *kiza* posture.
❿ Sit in the *seiza* posture.

Tai-Sabaki

What is important in technical training is how to use your body. You need to learn how to take a proper stance and a proper posture and how to use your body, and practice techniques repeatedly so that you can make use of what you have learned in technical training. In aikido training, we use the word *tori* to refer to one of the training pair who applies techniques and *uke* to the other on whom they are applied.

Irimi (against *tsuki*)

❶ *Tori* stands face to face with *uke*.
❷~❹ The instant *uke* brings his/her back foot forward to deliver a thrust, *tori* brings his/her front foot into *uke*'s rear side in an *irimi* movement and the back foot closer to him/herself to get out of the line of attack, and checks the thrust with his/her knife hand [*tegatana*].

The motion in Picture ❹ seen from a different angle
Tori steps into *uke*'s rear side in an *irimi* movement, getting out of the line of attack, and checks the thrust with his/her knife hand.

Irimi (against *shomen-uchi*)

❶ *Tori* stands face to face with *uke*.

❷ - ❺ The instant *uke* raises his/her knife hand to deliver a blow, *tori* brings his/her back foot extensively into *uke*'s rear side in an *irimi* movement, turns around, taking control of *uke*'s neck and knife hand, and draws back his/her front foot.

The motion in Picture ❺ seen from a different angle

Tori steps into *uke*'s rear side in an *irimi* movement and takes control of *uke*'s neck and knife hand.

Tenkan

❶ *Tori* and *uke* stand face to face with each other in a *gyaku-hanmi* stance.

❷ *Uke* grabs *tori*'s wrist in a *gyaku-hanmi* stance.

❸ *Tori* brings his/her front foot into *uke*'s rear side.

❹~❻ *Tori* pivots on the front foot and straightens his/her posture.

The motion in Pictures ❷~❻ seen from a different angle

Tenshin

❶ *Tori* and *uke* stand face to face with each other in an *ai-hanmi* stance.

❷~❹ The instant *uke* brings his/her back foot forward and raises his/her knife hand to deliver a side blow, *tori* brings his/her back foot diagonally forward, and checks *uke*'s knife-hand attack with his/her knife hand, delivering a (fake) blow [*atemi*] with the other hand.

❺ ~ ❽ *Tori* pivots on the foot he/she has brought forward, brings *uke*'s knife hand down with the *atemi* hand, and takes a *hanmi* stance.

The motion in Pictures ❸~❼ seen from a different angle

❶ ❷

Tenkai

❶ *Tori* and *uke* stand face to face with each other in a *gyaku-hanmi* stance.

❷ *Uke* grabs *tori*'s wrist in a *gyaku-hanmi* stance.

❸ *Tori* brings his/her knife hand sideways, bringing his/her front foot into *uke*'s rear side in an *irimi* movement, and delivers an *atemi* blow with the other hand.

❹~❻ *Tori* brings his/her back foot into *uke*'s rear side, bringing his/her knife hand upward, and makes an about-face.

The motion in Pictures ❸~❻ seen from a different angle

Ukemi

You need to practice *Ukemi* to prevent injuries.

Koho-hanten-ukemi

❶ Stand in a *hanmi* stance.

❷ Put the knee of your back leg onto the mat without tiptoeing.

❸〜❹ Put the knee, hip (on the same side), waist and back onto the mat in this order. When your back touches the mat, you pull in your chin as if to see your belt and tap the mat with the hand on the other side.

❺〜❻ Shift your weight forward, put your back, waist, and thighs onto the mat in this order, and stand up.

Koho-kaiten-ukemi

❶ Stand in a *hanmi* stance.
❷ Put the knee of your back leg onto the mat without tiptoeing.
❸~❹ Put the knee, hip (on the same side), waist and back onto the mat in this order.
❺ ~❽ Put your both hands on to the mat and straighten the upper part of your body. Put the diagonal line from one side of your hips to the other side of your shoulders onto the mat. Try consciously to make the shift of your weight effective.

*Beginners are advised to refrain from giving momentum to their movements in practicing this break-fall so that they may not hit their head hard on the mat. At first they can start from the kneeling position seen in Picture ❷ .

Zenpo-kaiten-ukemi

❶ Stand in a *hanmi* stance.

❷ Lower your body, bending both knees, and put the hand on the same side as your front leg onto the mat. (Turn your fingertips towards yourself in putting your hand onto the mat.)

❸~❼ Put the hand, arm, shoulder, back, waist, and the knee of your back leg onto the mat in this order and stand up.

At one point of this motion, tap the mat with the other hand, which touches the mat in its natural course.

Katame-waza-ukemi

❶~❹ *Tori* takes control of *uke*'s wrist and elbow and swings down *uke*'s arm in a circular motion. *Uke* loses balance in the upper body with the centre of gravity shifting to his/her back leg, keeps balance, bending his/her knees flexibly, and puts the other hand onto the mat.

❺~⓫ *Uke* puts the knee on the same side as the hand which has touched the mat and the other parts of his/her body one by one onto the mat and finally lies on his/her stomach. *Uke* slides the hand on the mat in lowering his/her upper body so as not to hit his/her face or chest hard on the mat.

Wrist Exercises

Since aikido has many wristlock techniques, it is important for trainees to do wrist exercises to make their wrists tough and flexible.

Wrist Exercise for *Dai-nikyo*

❶ Direct the thumb of your right hand downward and grab the back of the hand with your left hand, putting your left thumb on the base of your right thumb and holding the other side of your right hand with the other four fingers of your left hand.

❷ Press your arms towards the centre of your body, drawing both hands to your chest. Bend the wrist of your right hand to make it tough and flexible.

Wrist Exercise for *Kote-gaeshi*

❶ Direct the fingertips of both hands upward, put your right thumb between the bases of your left ring finger and little finger, and hold the side of your left thumb with the other four fingers of your right hand.

❷ Press your right hand against the left hand right in front of your body to turn it clockwise, thereby making it tough and flexible.

Back Stretching Exercise

This is a cool-down exercise after training.

❶ One of the training partners, whose back is to be stretched, grabs the other's wrists in a *gyaku-hanmi* stance.

❷~❹ The other of the partners brings his/her front foot forward, pivots in a *tenkan* movement, and swings up both arms, standing back to back with his/her partner.

❺ The latter of the partners bends both knees and lowers his/her waist, stretching both arms so much as to make them touch both ears.

❻ The latter lowers his/her waist farther, puts the former on his/her back, and stretches both arms. At this time, it is important for the former to relax.

Nage-waza

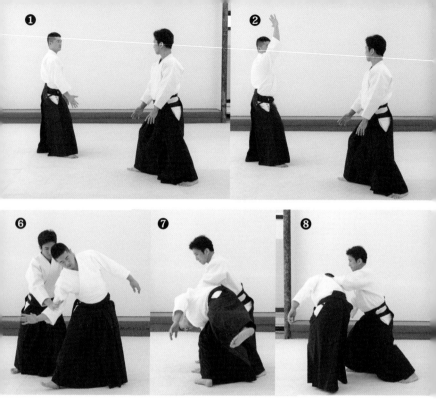

Irimi-nage

Irimi-nage is characterized by the bodily movement in which *tori*, getting out of the line of attack, slides into *uke*'s rear side. After sliding into *uke*'s rear side, *tori* pivots in a *tenkan* movement, taking control of *uke*'s neck and knife hand and steers *uke* in front of him/her. *Tori* then brings his/her back foot extensively forward, raising and curving his/her knife hand at the same time, and brings *uke* onto the mat.

Shomen-uchi Irimi-nage

❶ *Tori* stands face to face with *uke*.

❷~❺ The instant *uke* raises his/her hand to deliver a blow, *tori* brings his/her back foot extensively forward to step into *uke*'s rear side in an *irimi* movement, taking control of *uke*'s neck and knife hand. At this point, *tori* takes the same *hanmi* stance as *uke*, facing the same direction.

❻~❿ *Tori* pivots in a *tenkan* movement, bringing *uke* to the tip of his/her shoulder.

⓫~⓭ *Tori* brings his back foot extensively forward, swinging his/her upper hand down and bringing *uke* onto the mat.

Important Points to Remember in *Shomen-uchi Irimi-nage*

Tori brings his/her back foot forward as if to slide into the back of *uke*'s heels.

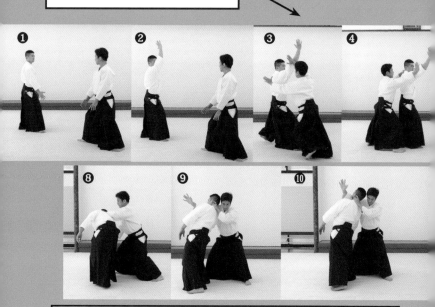

The motion in Pictures ❺∼❼ seen from a different angle
Tori brings *uke* to the tip of his/her shoulder in a *tenkan* movement with special attention to the point of contact between the two knife hands.

The close-up of Picture ❺

Tori draws the other foot to take a hanmi stance and faces the same direction as uke.

❺ ❻ ❼

⓫ ⓬ ⓭

The motion in Pictures ⓫～⓬ seen from a different angle
Tori brings his back foot extensively forward, swinging his/her upper hand down and bringing uke onto the mat.

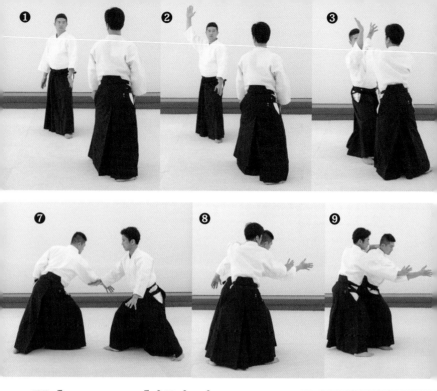

Yokomen-uchi Irimi-nage

❶ *Tori* stands face to face with *uke*.

❷～❹ The instant *uke* brings his/her foot forward to deliver a side blow, raising his/her knife hand, *tori* brings his/her back foot obliquely forward, checks the attack with his/her knife hand, and delivers an *atemi* blow with the other hand.

❺～❼ *Tori* pivots on his/her front foot, brings *uke*'s knife hand down with the *atemi* hand, and takes a *hanmi* stance.

❽～❾ *Tori* brings his back foot extensively to *uke*'s rear side in an *irimi* movement and takes control of *uke*'s knife hand and neck.

❿ - ⓬ *Tori* pivots in a *tenkan* movement, bringing *uke* to the tip of his/her shoulder.

⓭ - ⓯ *Tori* brings his back foot extensively forward, swinging his/her upper hand down and bringing *uke* onto the mat.

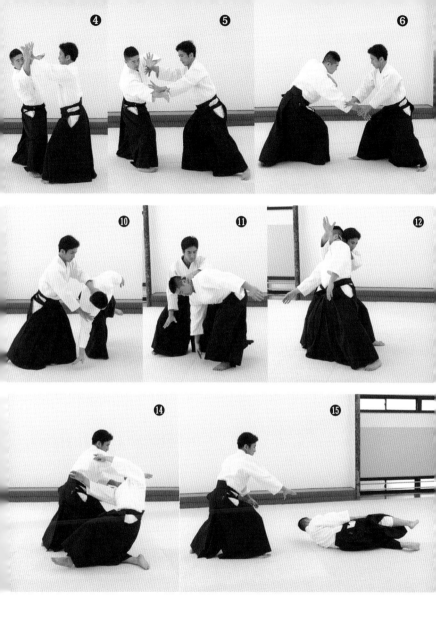

Katate-dori Irimi-nage (Ai-hanmi)

❶ *Tori* stands face to face with *uke*.

❷ *Uke* grabs *tori*'s wrist in an *ai-hanmi* stance.

❸~❺ *Tori* raises his/her knife hand, bringing his/her back foot to *uke*'s rear side in an *irimi* movement, and takes control of *uke*'s neck and knife hand.

❻~❽ *Tori* pivots in a *tenkan* movement, bringing *uke* to the tip of his/her shoulder.

❾~❷ *Tori* brings his back foot extensively forward, swinging his/her upper hand down and bringing *uke* onto the mat.

Important Points to Remember in *Katate-dori Irimi-nage (Ai-hanmi)*

The motion in Pictures ❷~❺ seen from a different angle
Tori raises his/her knife hand, bringing his/her back foot to *uke*'s rear side in an *irimi* movement, and takes control of *uke*'s neck and knife hand. After sliding into *uke*'s rear side in an *irimi* movement, *tori* faces the same direction as *uke*.

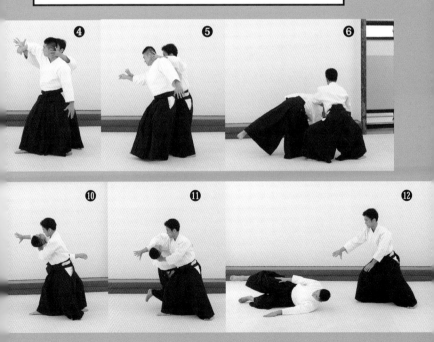

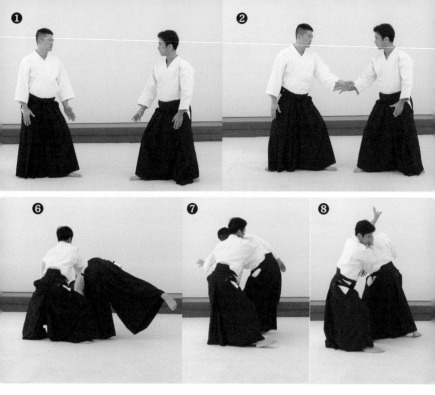

Katate-dori Irimi-nage (Gyaku-hanmi)

❶ *Tori* stands face to face with *uke*.

❷ *Uke* grabs *tori*'s wrist in a *gyaku-hanmi* stance.

❸~❹ *Tori* brings his/her front foot farther into *uke*'s rear side, putting the free hand between *uke*'s and his/her arms and separating their hands, and takes control of *uke*'s neck and knife hand.

❺ - ❽ *Tori* pivots in a *tenkan* movement and brings *uke* to the tip of his/her shoulder.

❾ - ⓭ *Tori* brings his back foot extensively forward, swinging his/her upper hand down and bringing *uke* onto the mat.

Important Points to Remember in *Katate-dori Irimi-nage (Gyaku-hanmi)*

The close-up of Pictures ❷~❹
Tori slides into *uke*'s rear side, puts his/her free hand between *uke*'s and his/her arms, rotates, and separates *uke*'s hand.

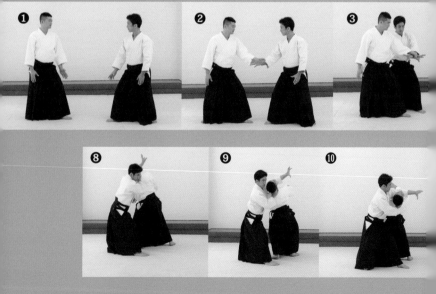

Shiho-nage

Shiho-nage is one of the representative techniques of aikido in which 'the reason of the sword is projected upon the body'. *Tori* swings both arms upward and brings *uke* down onto the mat.

Katate-dori Shiho-nage (Gyaku-hanmi) Omote

❶ *Tori* stands face to face with *uke*.

❷~❸ When *uke* grabs *tori*'s wrist in a *gyaku-hanmi* stance, *tori* brings his/her back foot forward, raising his/her knife hand, and put the other hand on *uke*'s wrist.

❹~❻ *Tori* takes another step forward, raising his/her arms, turns around, and takes control of *uke*'s hand with both hands.

❼~❿ *Tori* swings both arms downward, bringing *uke* onto the mat.

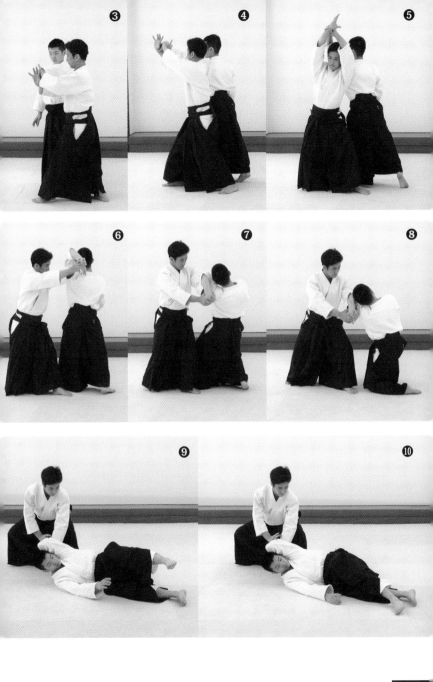

The motion in Pictures ❷～❺ seen from a different angle
When *uke* grabs *tori*'s wrist in a *gyaku-hanmi* stance, *tori* brings his/her back foot forward, raising his/her knife hand, and put the other hand on *uke*'s wrist.

Important Points to Remember in
Katate-dori Shiho-nage (Gyaku-hanmi)Omote

The motion in Pictures ❺～❼ seen from a different angle
Tori turns around, takes control of *uke*'s hand with both hands, and swings both arms downward, bringing *uke* onto the mat.

Tori takes another step forward, raising his/her arms, turns around, and takes control of uke's hand with both hands.

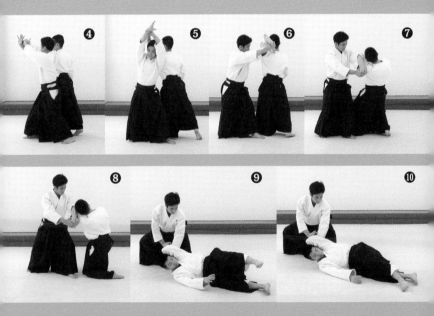

Katate-dori Shiho-nage (Gyaku-hanmi) Ura

❶ *Tori* stands face to face with *uke*.

❷ *Uke* grabs *tori*'s wrist in a *gyaku-hanmi* stance.

❸~❼ *Tori* brings his/her front foot into *uke*'s rear side, raising his/her knife hand and putting the other hand on *uke*'s wrist, and pivots in a *tenkan* movement, swinging both arms upward.

❽ ~❿ *Tori* turns around and takes control of *uke*'s hand with both hands.

⓫ ~ ⓭ *Tori* brings *uke* down onto the mat.

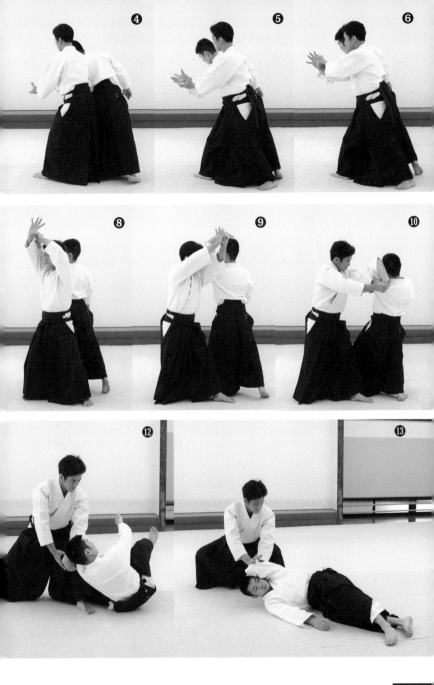

Important Points to Remember in
Katate-dori Shiho-nage (Gyaku-hanmi)Ura

The motion in Pictures ❷~❽ seen from a different angle
In making a series of bodily movements of *irimi* and *tenkan* at *uke*'s rear side, *tori* needs to make sure that his/her grabbed hand should always stay right in front of his/her body.

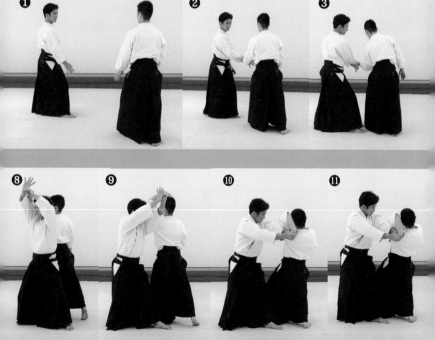

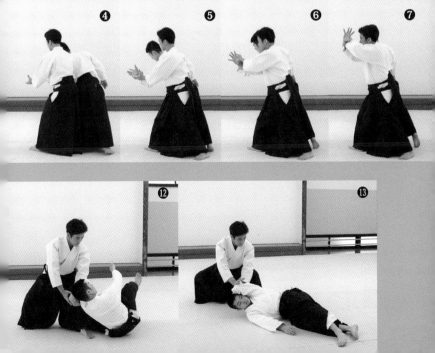

Hanmi-handachi
Katate-dori Shiho-nage

❶ *Tori* sits face to face with *uke*.

❷~❸ When *uke* grabs *tori*'s wrist in a *gyaku-hanmi* stance, *tori* half rises, raising his/her knife hand, to put the other hand on *uke*'s wrist.

❹ *Tori* raises one of his/her knees that is closer to *uke*, swinging his/her knife hand upward.

❺~❻ *Tori* turns around and takes control of *uke*'s hand.

❼~❾ *Tori* brings *uke* down onto the mat.

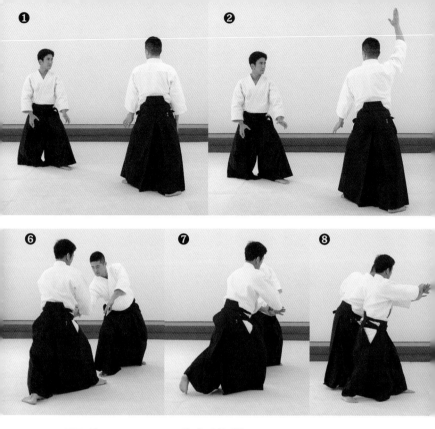

Yokomen-uchi Shiho-nage

Omote

❶ *Tori* stands face to face with *uke*.

❷~❹ The instant *uke* brings his/her back foot forward to deliver a side blow at *tori*, *tori* brings his/her back foot obliquely aside, swinging both knife hands upward, and takes control of *uke*'s knife hand with one of his/her knife hands, delivering an *atemi* blow with the other.

❺~❽ *Tori* rotates in a *tenshin* movement, bringing *uke*'s knife hand downward, and takes control of *uke*'s wrist with both hands.

❾~❿ *Tori* brings his/her back foot extensively forward, swinging both arms upward, and turns around to take control of *uke*'s hand.

⓫~⓭ *Tori* brings *uke* down onto the mat.

Important Points to Remember in
Yokomen-uchi Shiho-nage Omote

The motion in Pictures ❸~❻ seen from a different angle
Tori takes control of *uke*'s knife hand with one of his/her knife hands, delivering an *atemi* blow with the other. *Tori* rotates in a *tenshin* movement, bringing *uke*'s knife hand downward, and takes control of *uke*'s wrist with both hands.

❶ ❷ ❸

❼ ❽ ❾ ❿

The motion in Pictures ❼ - ❾ seen from a different angle
Tori brings his/her back foot extensively forward, swinging both arms right in front of his/her body, and turns around.

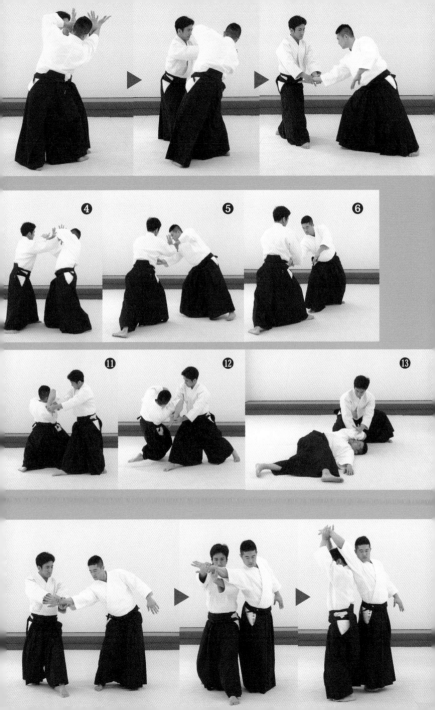

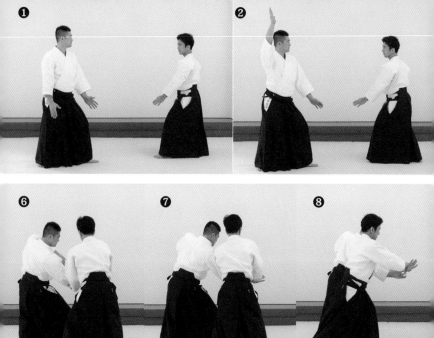

Yokomen-uchi Shiho-nage Ura

❶ *Tori* stands face to face with *uke*.

❷～❹ The instant *uke* brings his/her back foot forward to deliver a side blow at *tori*, *tori* brings his/her front foot into *uke*'s rear side in an *irimi* movement, delivering an *atemi* blow with one of his/her knife hands and taking control of *uke*'s knife hand with the other.

❺～❾ *Tori* brings *uke*'s knife hand downward, grabs *uke*'s hand with both hands, and swings both arms upward, pivoting in a *tenkan* movement.

❿～⓮ *Tori* turns around, taking control of *uke*'s hand, and brings *uke* down onto the mat.

Important Points to Remember in *Yokomen-uchi Shiho-nage Ura*

❶　　　　　❷

❼　　❽　　❾　　❿　　⓫

The motion in Pictures ❸~❽ seen from two different angles

Tori brings his/her front foot into *uke*'s rear side in an *irimi* movement, delivering an *atemi* blow with one of his/her knife hands and taking control of *uke*'s knife hand with the other. *Tori* brings *uke*'s knife hand downward, grabs *uke*'s hand with both hands, and swings both arms upward, pivoting in a *tenkan* movement.

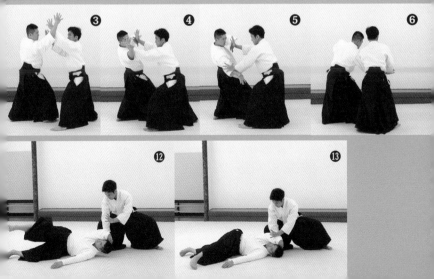

❸   ❹   ❺   ❻

⓬   ⓭

Tenchi-nage

This is a technique in which *tori* slides into *uke*'s rear side, bringing his/her knife hands apart at the same time, one upward and the other downward, in a spiral motion.

Ryote-dori Tenchi-nage

Omote

❶ *Tori* stands face to face with *uke*.

❷ *Uke* grabs *tori* by both hands in an *ai-hanmi* stance.

❸~❺ *Tori* brings his/her back foot extensively into *uke*'s rear side, bringing both knife hands apart, one upward and the other downward.

❻~❽ *Tori* brings his/her back foot farther forward, turning both knife hands inward, and turns his/her upper hand downward, bringing *uke* down onto the mat.

Important Points to Remember in
Ryote-dori Tenchi-nage Omote

The motion in Pictures ❷～❻ seen from a different angle
Tori brings his/her back foot extensively into *uke*'s rear side, bringing both knife hands apart, one upward and the other downward. *Tori* brings his/her back foot farther forward, turning both knife hands inward, and turns his/her upper hand downward, bringing *uke* down onto the mat.

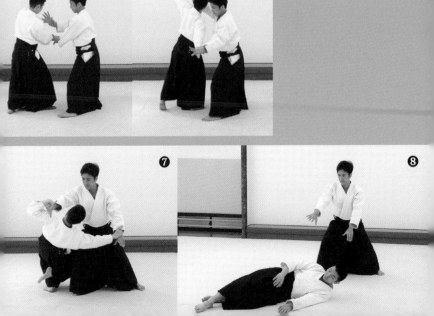

Ryote-dori Tenchi-nage Ura

❶ *Tori* stands face to face with *uke*.

❷ *Uke* grabs *tori* by both hands in a *gyaku-hanmi* stance.

❸~❼ *Tori* brings his/her front foot into *uke*'s rear side, pivots on the foot in a *tenkan* movement, bringing both knife hands apart, one upward and the other downward, and steers *uke* in front of him/her.

❽ ~ ⓬ *Tori* brings his/her back foot farther forward, turning both knife hands inward, and turns his/her upper hand downward, bringing *uke* down onto the mat.

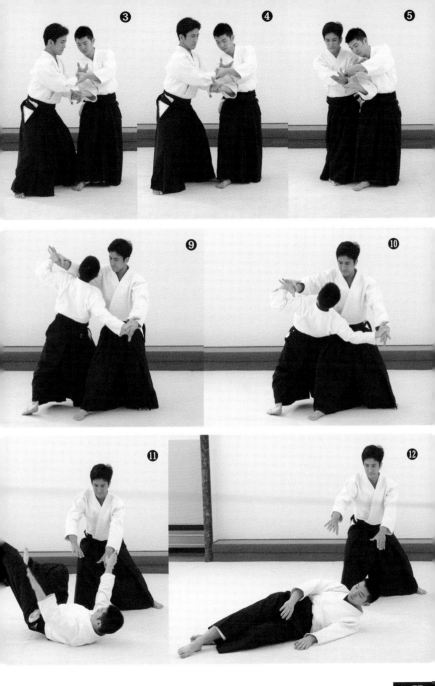

The close-up motion of hands in Picture ❷～❿
Tori brings both knife hands apart, one upward and the other downward, in a *tenkan* movement, steers *uke* in front of him, turns both knife hands inward, and turns the upper hand downward, bringing *uke* down onto the mat.

Important Points to Remember in
Ryote-dori Tenchi-nage Ura

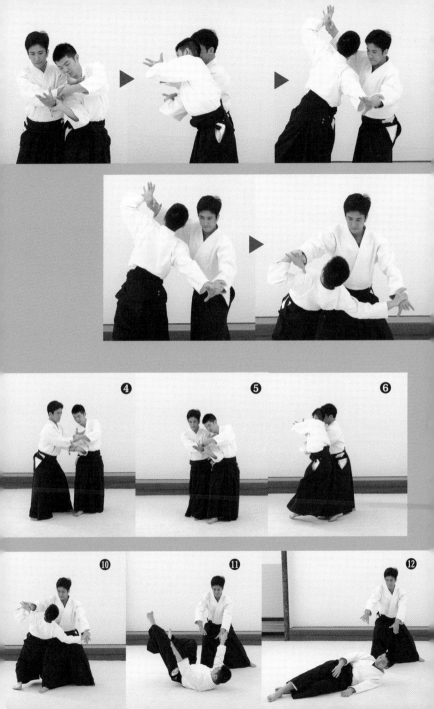

Kaiten-nage

Katate-dori Kaiten-nage Uchi-kaiten

❶ *Tori* stands face to face with *uke*.

❷ *Uke* grabs *tori*'s wrist in a *gyaku-hanmi* stance.

❸ *Tori* brings his/her front foot obliquely forward, bringing down his/her knife hand obliquely forward and delivering an *atemi* blow with the other hand.

❹～❻ *Tori* brings his/her back foot into *uke*'s rear side, swinging his/her knife hand upward, and turns around.

❼～❾ *Tori* brings his/her front foot backward, swinging down his/her knife hand, and draws out *uke*'s arm by the wrist, taking control of the back of *uke*'s neck with the other hand.

❿～⓭ *Tori* brings his/her back foot forward and at the same time thrusts *uke*'s arm forward, bringing *uke* down onto the mat.

The motion in Pictures ❽～❾ seen from a different angle
Tori draws out *uke*'s arm by the wrist with one of his/her hands and takes control of the back of *uke*'s neck with the other.

Important Points to Remember in *Katate-dori Kaiten-nage Uchi-kaiten*

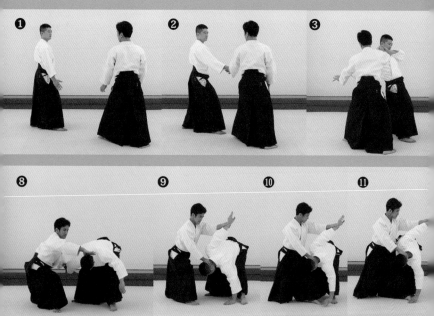

Katate-dori Kaiten-nage
Soto-kaiten

❶ *Tori* stands face to face with *uke*.

❷ *Uke* grabs *tori*'s wrist in a *gyaku-hanmi* stance.

❸～❹ *Tori* brings his/her front foot obliquely forward, bringing down his/her knife hand obliquely forward and delivering an *atemi* blow with the other hand.

❺～❻ *Tori* swings his/her knife hand upward in such a way that it is pressed on *uke*'s wrist and turns around.

❼～❶ *Tori* brings his/her front foot backward, draws out *uke*'s arm by the wrist, taking another step backward, and takes control of the back of *uke*'s neck with the other hand.

❶❷～❶❺ *Tori* brings his/her back foot forward and thrusts *uke*'s arm forward, bringing *uke* down onto the mat.

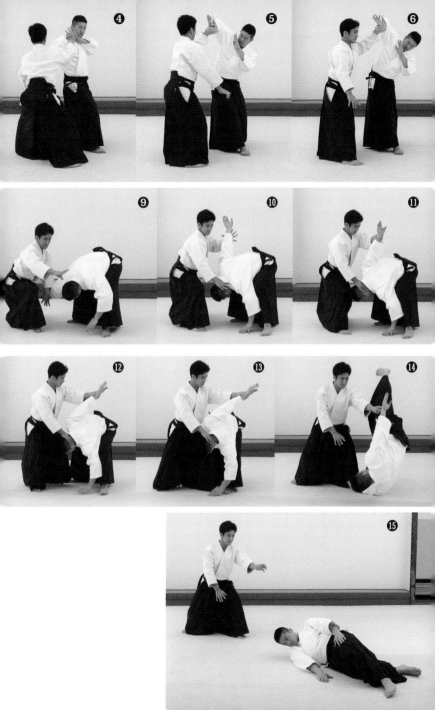

Important Points to Remember in *Katate-dori Kaiten-nage Soto-kaiten*

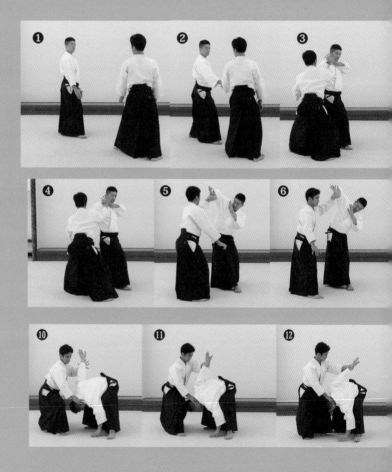

The close-up of the motion in Pictures ❺～❼
Tori swings his/her knife hand upward in such a way that it is pressed on *uke*'s wrist and turns around.

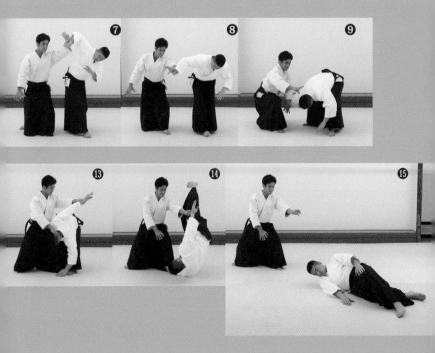

Nage-katame-waza

Kote-gaeshi

This is a technique in which throwing and grappling techniques are combined. The main technique is *kote-gaeshi*, in which *tori* throws *uke* and pins him/her down in the *nikyo* hold. Trainees are advised to take care to keep flowing the sequence of movement of throwing and grappling.

Ttsuki Kote-gaeshi

❶ *Tori* stands face to face with *uke*.

❷～❸ The instant *uke* brings his/her back foot forward to deliver a thrust, *tori* brings his/her front foot into *uke*'s rear side, taking control of *uke*'s arm with his/her knife hand.

❹～❻ *Tori* grabs *uke*'s hand with the hand that has taken control of his/her arm and steers *uke* in front of him/her, pivoting in a *tenkan* movement.

❼ ～ ⓫ *Tori* brings his/her front foot aside, twisting *uke*'s hand, brings his/her back foot forward, putting the other hand on the back of *uke*'s hand, and brings *uke* down onto the mat with both hands.

⓬ ～ ⓰ *Tori* takes control of *uke*'s hand and elbow and holds him/her facedown.

⓱ ～ ⓳ *Tori* takes the *kiza* posture, putting *uke*'s shoulder between both knees, and pins him/her down in the *nikyo* hold.

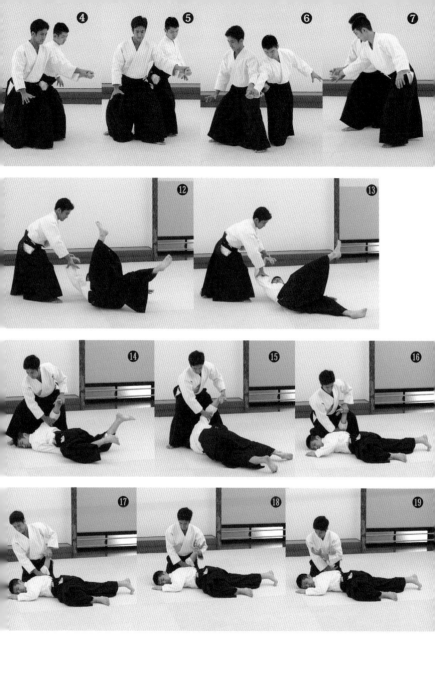

Important Points to Remember in *Ttsuki Kote-gaeshi*

❶ ❷ ❸ ❹

❾ ❿ ⓫ ⓬

The motion in Pictures ❹～❿ seen from a different angle

Tori grabs *uke*'s hand with the hand that has taken control of *uke*'s arm and pivots in a *tenkan* movement, steering *uke* in front of him/her. *Tori* then brings his/her front foot aside, twisting *uke*'s hand, brings his/her back foot forward, putting the other hand on the back of *uke*'s hand (curling its fingertips), and brings *uke* down onto the mat with both hands.

The motion in Pictures ❷∼❹ seen from a different angle
Tori takes control of *uke*'s arm with his/her knife hand and grabs *uke*'s hand with the same hand.

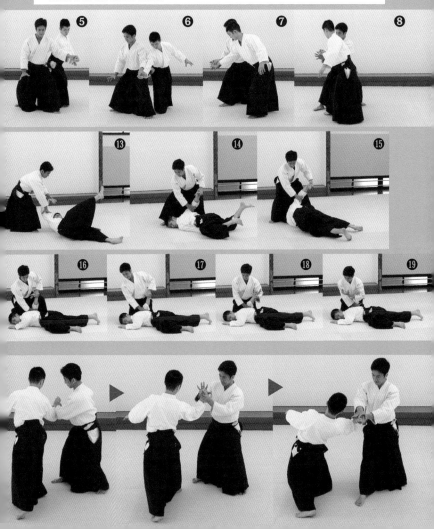

Shomen-uchi Kote-gaeshi

❶ *Tori* stands face to face with *uke*.

❷~❼ The instant *uke* raises his/her hand to deliver a front blow, *tori* brings his/her front foot into *uke*'s rear side in an *irimi* movement and pivots in a *tenkan* movement, taking control of *uke*'s hand.

❽~❾ *Tori* grabs *uke*'s hand with the hand that has taken control of *uke*'s arm and steers *uke* in front of him/her.

❿~⓮ *Tori* brings his/her front foot aside, twisting *uke*'s hand, brings his/her back foot forward, putting the other hand on the back of *uke*'s hand, and brings *uke* down onto the mat with both hands.

⓯ - ⓳ *Tori* turns over *uke* facedown, taking control of *uke*'s hand and elbow, and pins *uke* down with his/her shoulder between both knees.

Important Points to Remember in *Shomen-uchi Kote-gaeshi*

The close-up of the motion in Pictures ⑮～⑲

Tori turns over *uke* facedown, taking control of his/her hand and elbow, and pins *uke* down, pressing the arm close to his/her body and locking the shoulder joint.

**The motion in Picture ❻
seen from a different angle**

Tori puts his/her thumb between the bases of *uke*'s ring finger and little finger and holds the inside of *uke*'s thumb with the other four fingers.

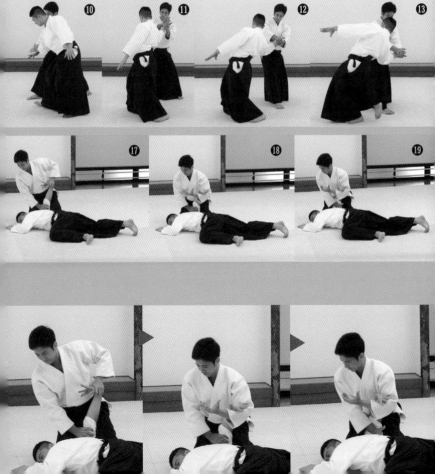

Katate-dori Kote-gaeshi

❶ *Tori* stands face to face with *uke*.

❷ *Uke* grabs *tori*'s wrist in a *gyaku-hanmi* stance.

❸ ~ ❻ *Tori* brings his/her front foot into *uke*'s rear side in an *irimi* movement, putting his/her free hand between *uke*'s and his/her arms and separating their hands, and takes control of *uke*'s hand.

❼ ~ ❾ *Tori* grabs *uke*'s hand with the other hand and steers *uke* in front of him/her.

❿ ~ ⓭ *Tori* brings his/her front foot aside, twisting *uke*'s hand, brings his/her back foot forward, putting the other hand on the back of *uke*'s hand, and brings *uke* down onto the mat with both hands.

⓮ ~ ⓲ *Tori* turns over *uke* facedown, taking control of *uke*'s hand and elbow, and pins *uke* down with his/her shoulder between both knees.

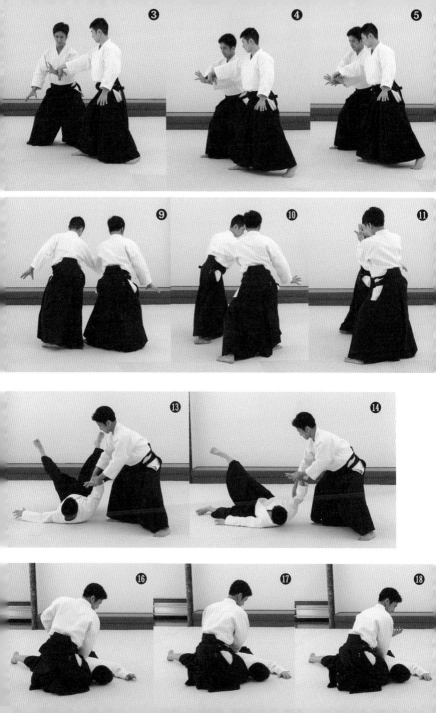

Important Points to Remember in *Katate-dori Kote-gaeshi*

The close-up of the motion in Pictures ❸〜❼
Tori puts his/her free hand between *uke*'s and his/her arms, separates their hands, and holds *uke*'s hand.

Katame-waza

Dai-ikkyo

This is a technique that constitutes the basis for grappling techniques of aikido, which all start from *dai-ikkyo*.

Shomen-uchi Dai-ikkyo Omote

❶ *Tori* stands face to face with *uke*.

❷~⓫ The instant *uke* raises his/her knife hand, *tori* brings his/her front foot obliquely forward in an *irimi* movement, taking control of *uke*'s wrist and elbow, swings *uke*'s arm down, and brings his/her back foot forward.

⓬~⓭ *Tori* pins *uke* facedown.

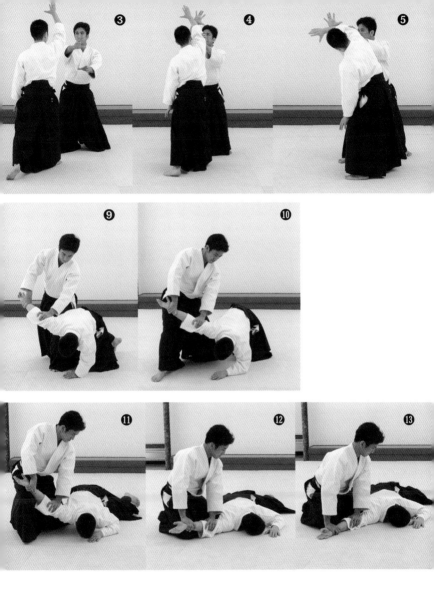

Important Points to Remember in *Shomen-uchi Dai-ikkyo Omote*

The motion in Picture ⓭ seen from a different angle

Tori pins *uke* down so that *uke*'s arm and side may form an obtuse angle. *Tori* presses his/her inner knee on *uke*'s side and outer knee by *uke*'s wrist and pins *uke* down, placing his/her weight on *uke*'s wrist and elbow that he/she is holding.

The motion in Pictures ❸~❽ seen from a different angle
Tori takes control of *uke*'s wrist and elbow, twists his/her waist, swings *uke*'s arm down, and brings his/her back foot forward.

❺ ❻

⓫ ⓬ ⓭

The motion in Picture ⓭ seen from another angle
Tori takes the *kiza* posture and pins *uke* facedown.

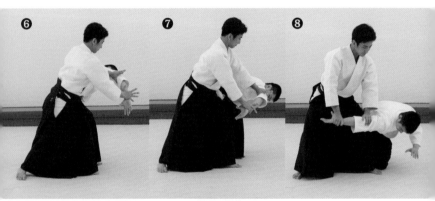

Shomen-uchi Dai-ikkyo Ura

❶ *Tori* stands face to face with *uke*.

❷∼❿ The instant *uke* raises his/her knife hand, *tori* brings his/her front foot obliquely forward in an *irimi* movement, taking control of *uke*'s wrist and elbow, and pivots in a *tenkan* movement, swinging *uke*'s arm down.

⓫∼⓬ *Tori* pins *uke* facedown.

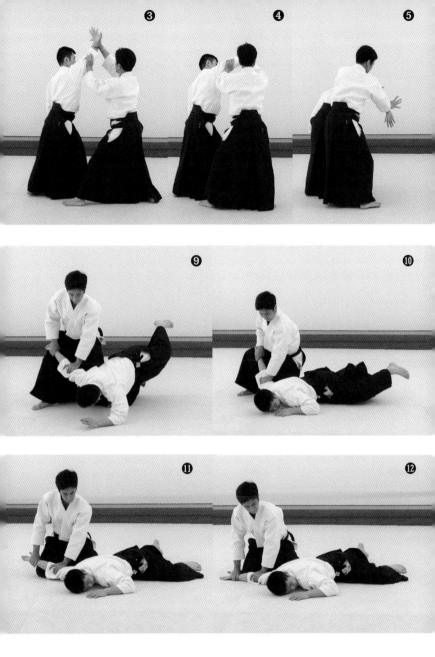

Important Points to Remember in *Shomen-uchi Dai-ikkyo Ura*

The motion in Pictures ❸～❽ seen from a different angle
Tori slides into *uke*'s rear side in an *irimi* movement, taking control of *uke*'s wrist, and pivots in a *tenkan* movement, swinging *uke*'s arm down.

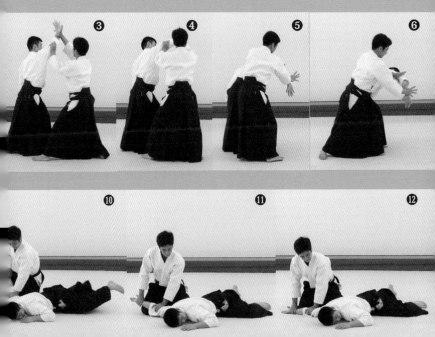

❶ ❷

Shomen-uchi Dai-ikkyo Zagi Omote

❶ *Tori* sits face to face with *uke*.

❷ ～ ❼ The instant *uke* raises his/her knife hand, *tori* takes control of *uke*'s wrist and elbow, bringing his/her front knee slightly aside, swings *uke*'s arm, and goes forward by knee-walking.

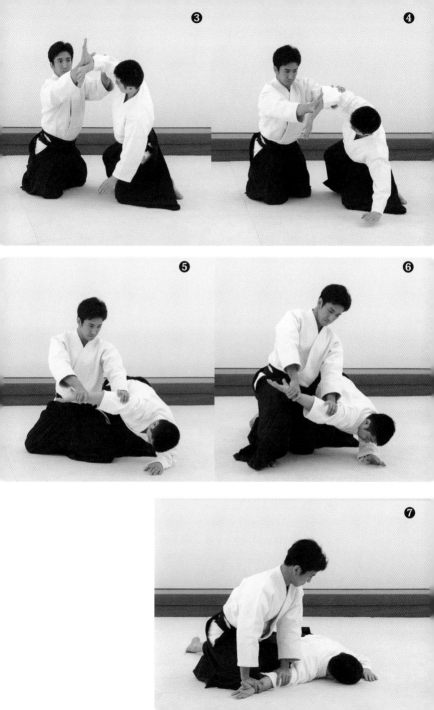

Shomen-uchi Dai-ikkyo Zagi Ura

❶ *Tori* sits face to face with *uke*.

❷ ～❽ The instant *uke* raises his/her knife hand, *tori* brings his/her front knee into *uke*'s rear side in an *irimi* movement, taking control of *uke*'s wrist and elbow. *Tori* pivots in a *tenkan* movement, swinging *uke*'s arm down.

❾ ～❿ *Tori* pins *uke* facedown in the *kiza* posture.

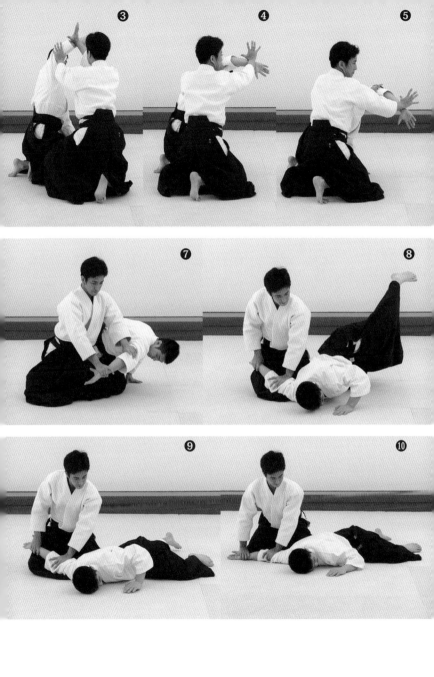

Katate-dori Dai-ikkyo (Ai-hanmi) Omote

❶ *Tori* stands face to face with *uke*.

❷ ~ ❻ The instant *uke* grabs *tori*'s wrist in an *ai-hanmi* stance, *tori* raises his/her knife hand, brings his/her front foot obliquely forward in an *irimi* movement, swinging the knife hand upward, and takes control of *uke*'s elbow with the other hand.

❼ ~ ❿ *Tori* brings his/her back foot forward, swinging *uke*'s arm down.

⓫ ~ ⓯ *Tori* steps farther forward and pins *uke* facedown onto the mat.

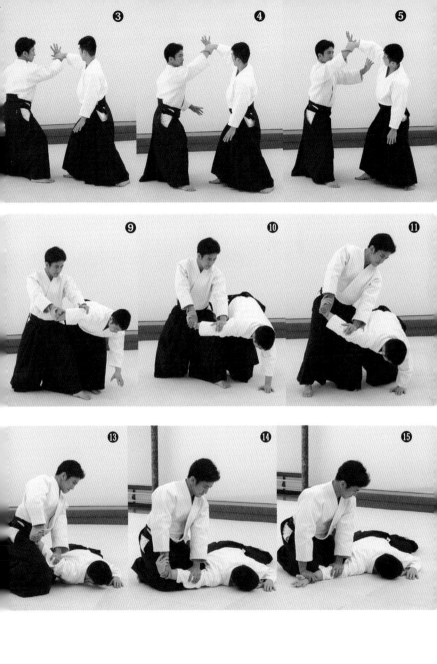

Katate-dori Dai-ikkyo
(Ai-hanmi) Ura

❶ *Tori* stands face to face with *uke*.

❷ ~ ❺ The instant *uke* grabs *tori*'s wrist in an *ai-hanmi* stance, *tori* raises his/her knife hand, brings his/her back foot into *uke*'s rear side in an *irimi* movement, and takes control of *uke*'s elbow with the other hand.

❻ ~ ❿ *Tori* swings *uke*'s arm down in an *tenkan* movement.

⓬ *Tori* pins *uke* facedown onto the mat.

Dai-nikyo

Dai-nikyo is a technique which has wrist- and shoulder-locking movements in addition to *dai-ikkyo*. It is characterized by the way *tori* takes control of *uke*'s wrist and shoulder, and trainees are advised to practice the movements repeatedly.

Shomen-uchi Dai-nikyo Omote

❶ *Tori* stands face to face with *uke*.

❷～❽ The instant *uke* brings his/her front foot and raises his/her knife hand, *tori* brings his/her front foot obliquely forward in an *irimi* movement, taking control of *uke*'s wrist and elbow, twists his/her waist to bring his/her back foot forward, swinging *uke*'s arm down, and turns and grabs *uke*'s hand.

❾～⓫ *Tori* takes another step forward to bring *uke* facedown onto the mat and puts *uke*'s shoulder between both knees in the *kiza* posture.

⓬～⓮ *Tori* presses *uke*'s arm to his/her body with both arms, locking the shoulder.

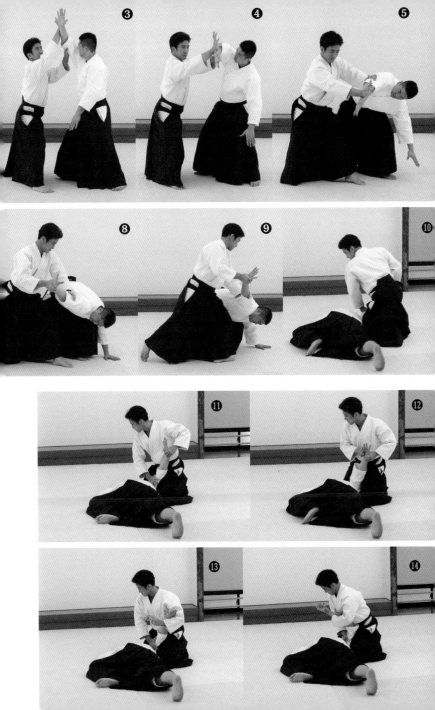

Important Points to Remember *in Shomen-uchi Dai-nikyo Omote*

❶ ❷ ❸

❼ ❽ ❾ ❿

The motion in Pictures ❿～⓮ seen from a different angle
Tori steps forward to bring *uke* facedown onto the mat, puts *uke*'s shoulder between both knees in the *kiza* posture, and presses *uke*'s arm to his/her body with both arms, locking the shoulder.

The motion in Pictures ❺~❽ seen from a different angle

Tori opens his/her hand, puts it on *uke*'s wrist, and turns and grabs the hand, locking the wrist.

Shomen-uchi Dai-nikyo Ura

❶ *Tori* stands face to face with *uke*.

❷～❹ The instant *uke* brings his/her front foot and raises his/her knife hand, *tori* brings his/her back foot into *uke*'s rear side in an *irimi* movement, taking control of *uke*'s elbow and knife hand.

❺～❼ *Tori* swings *uke*'s arm down in a *tenkan* movement and takes control of *uke*'s elbow with one hand, turning and grabbing *uke*'s hand with the other.

❽～⓫ *Tori* puts *uke*'s hand on the tip of his/her shoulder, bends *uke*'s wrist and elbow joint, and locks the wrist joint.

⓬～⓱ *Tori* takes control of *uke*'s hand and elbow, pinning *uke* facedown onto the mat, and locks *uke*'s shoulder joint.

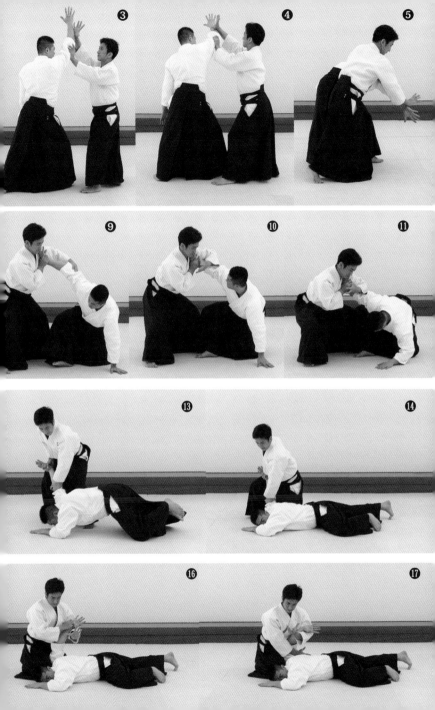

Important Points to Remember in Shomen-uchi Dai-nikyo Ura

The motion in Picture ❻ seen from a different angle

Tori takes control of *uke*'s elbow with one hand, turning and grabbing *uke*'s hand with the other hand.

❹ ❺ ❻ ❼

⓫ ⓬ ⓭

The motion in Pictures ❽～⓫ seen from a different angle

Tori puts *uke*'s hand on the tip of his/her shoulder, bends *uke*'s wrist and elbow joint, and locks the wrist joint.

Kata-dori Dai-nikyo Omote

❶ *Tori* stands face to face with *uke*.

❷ ~ ❺ The instant *uke* grabs the tip of *tori*'s shoulder, *tori* brings his/her back foot aside, delivering an *atemi* blow, and makes a *tenshin* movement, bringing *uke*'s arm down with the *atemi* hand.

❻ ~ ❿ *Tori* takes control of *uke*'s hand with one hand and *uke*'s elbow with the other and swings *uke*'s arm up and then down in a circular motion.

⓫ ~ ⓭ *Tori* steps forward and pins *uke* facedown.

⓮ ~ ⓰ *Tori* takes the *kiza* posture to put *uke*'s shoulder between both knees and locks *uke*'s shoulder joint.

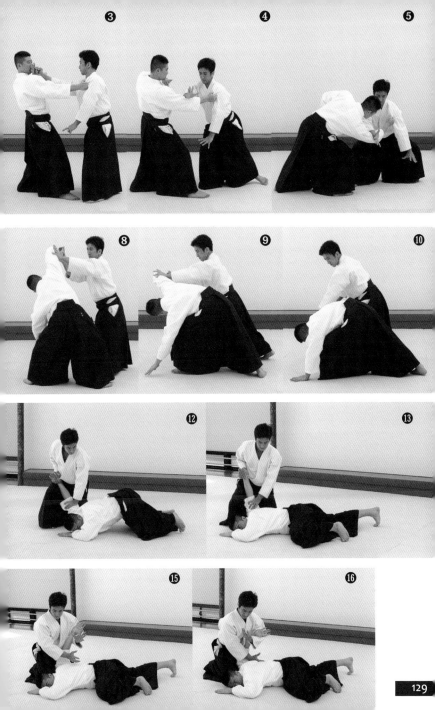

Important Points to Remember in *Kata-dori Dai-nikyo Omote*

The close-up of the motion in Pictures ❸～❿

Tori brings *uke*'s arm down with the *atemi* hand. *Tori* takes control of *uke*'s hand with that hand and *uke*'s elbow with the other and swings *uke*'s arm up and then down in a circular motion.

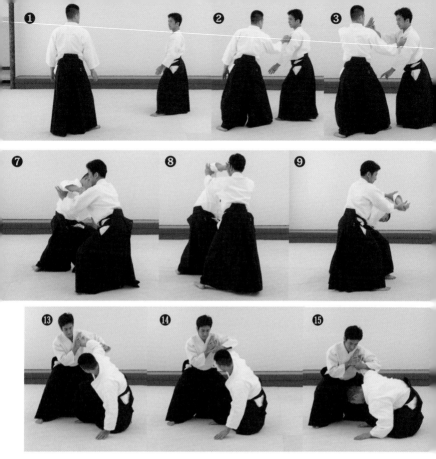

Kata-dori Dai-nikyo Ura

❶ *Tori* stands face to face with *uke*.

❷~❸ The instant *uke* grabs the tip of *tori*'s shoulder, *tori* delivers an *atemi* blow.

❹ ~ ❺ *Tori* takes a step into *uke*'s rear side and brings *uke*'s arm down with the *atemi* hand.

❻ ~ ⓫ *Tori* takes control of *uke*'s hand with that hand and *uke*'s elbow with the other and swings *uke*'s arm up and then down in a circular motion in a *tenkan* movement.

⓬ ~⓯ *Tori* puts *uke*'s hand on the tip of his/her shoulder, bends *uke*'s wrist and elbow joint, and locks the wrist joint.

⓰ ~ ⓴ *Tori* brings *uke* facedown onto the mat in a *tenkan* movement and locks *uke*'s shoulder joint.

The close-up of the motion in Pictures ❸～⓮

Tori delivers an *atemi* blow and brings *uke*'s arm down with the *atemi* hand. *Tori* then takes control of *uke*'s hand with that hand and *uke*'s elbow with the other and swings *uke*'s arm up and then down in a circular motion in a *tenkan* movement. *Tori* puts *uke*'s hand on the tip of his/her shoulder, bends *uke*'s wrist and elbow joint, and locks the wrist joint.

Important Points to Remember in *Kata-dori Dai-nikyo Ura*

❺   ❻   ❼   ❽

⓭   ⓮   ⓯   ⓰

⓳   ⓴

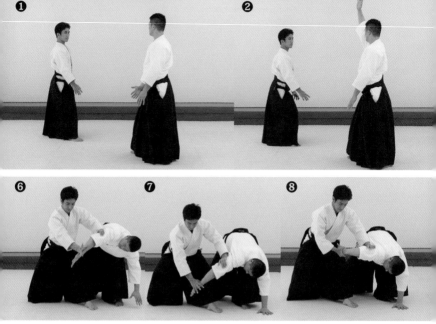

Dai-sankyo

Dai-sankyo is a technique which has wrist-, elbow-, and shoulder-locking movements in addition to *dai-ikkyo*. It comprises such complicated methods for changing grips and bodily movements that trainees are advised to practice it repeatedly.

Shomen-uchi Dai-sankyo Omote

❶ *Tori* stands face to face with *uke*.

❷ ～ ❻ The instant *uke* raises his/her knife hand, *tori* brings his/her front foot obliquely forward in an *irimi* movement to take control of *uke*'s elbow and knife hand and swings *uke*'s arm down, bringing his/her back foot forward.

❼ ～ ❽ *Tori* twists *uke*'s hand from outside to inside.

❾ ～ ❿ *Tori* grabs the back of *uke*'s hand with the hand which has taken control of *uke*'s elbow and swings the arm down.

⓫ ～ ⓮ *Tori* draws his/her back foot a bit closer and takes control of *uke*'s elbow with the other hand, pivoting in a *tenkan* movement.

⓯ ～ ⓱ *Tori* sits in the *kiza* posture with *uke*'s shoulder between both knees, changes the grip from one hand to the other, and locks *uke*'s shoulder joint.

Important Points to Remember in *Shomen-uchi Dai-sankyo Omote*

❶   ❷   ❸

❽   ❾   ❿   ⓫

⓰   ⓱

The motion in Pictures ❻～❿ seen from a different angle

Tori twists *uke*'s hand from outside to inside, grabs the back of *uke*'s hand with the hand which has taken control of *uke*'s elbow, and swings the arm down.

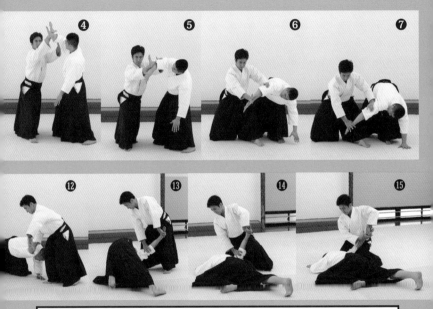

❹ ❺ ❻ ❼

⓬ ⓭ ⓮ ⓯

The motion in Pictures ⓮～⓱ seen from a different angle

Tori sits in the *kiza* posture with *uke*'s shoulder between both knees, changes the grip from one hand to the other, and locks *uke*'s shoulder joint.

Shomen-uchi Dai-sankyo Ura

❶ *Tori* stands face to face with *uke*.

❷ The instant *uke* brings his/her front foot forward and raises his/her knife hand, *tori* brings his/her back foot into *uke*'s rear side in an *irimi* movement, taking control of *uke*'s elbow and knife hand.

❸~❿ *Tori* swings *uke*'s arm down in a *tenkan* movement and twists *uke*'s hand from outside to inside with the hand which has been put on *uke*'s wrist. *Tori* also grabs the back of *uke*'s hand with the hand which has taken control of *uke*'s elbow.

⓫~⓭ *Tori* brings his/her front foot into *uke*'s rear side, takes control of *uke*'s elbow with the former hand, and brings *uke* facedown onto the mat in a *tenkan* movement.

⓮~⓰ *Tori* sits in the *kiza* posture with *uke*'s shoulder between both knees, changes the grip from one hand to the other, and locks *uke*'s shoulder joint.

Important Points to Remember in *Shomen-uchi Dai-sankyo Ura*

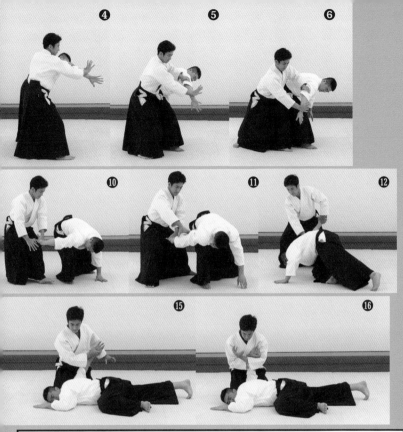

The close-up of the motion in Pictures ❽～❹

Tori twists *uke*'s hand and grabs its back with the hand which has taken control of *uke*'s elbow. *Tori* then brings his/her front foot into *uke*'s rear side, takes control of *uke*'s elbow with the former hand, brings *uke* facedown onto the mat in a *tenkan* movement, and locks *uke*'s shoulder joint.

Ushiro-ryotekubi-dori Dai-sankyo Omote

❶ *Tori* stands face to face with *uke*.

❷～**❹** *Uke* brings *tori*'s knife hand down and moves around to his/her rear. When *tori* brings his/her back foot forward, *uke* grabs *tori*'s both wrists.

❺～**❼** *Tori* swings both knife hands upward in a spiral motion.

❽～**⓬** *Tori* brings his/her front foot backward to bring both knife hands down and grabs the back of *uke*'s hand with the inner hand and its four fingers with the other.

⓭～**⓰** *Tori* brings his/her back foot forward to swing *uke*'s hand down, then brings his/her back foot to *uke*'s front, takes control of *uke*'s elbow with the latter hand, and bring *uke* facedown onto the mat in a *tenkan* movement.

⓱～**⓳** *Tori* sits in the *kiza* posture with *uke*'s shoulder between both knees, changes the grip from one hand to the other, and locks *uke*'s shoulder joint.

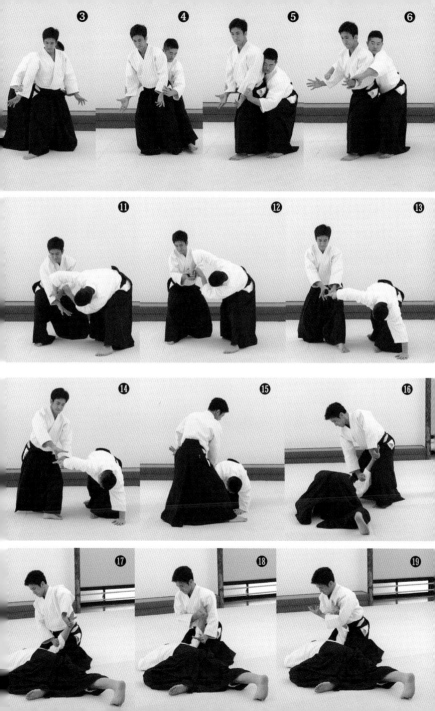

Important Points to Remember in *Ushiro-ryotekubi-dori Dai-sankyo Omote*

The motion in Pictures ❺~⓫ seen from a different angle

Tori swings both knife hands upward to lift *uke*'s upper body, brings his/her front foot backward, swinging both arms down, and grabs *uke*'s hand with his/her inner hand.

❹   ❺

❿   ⓫

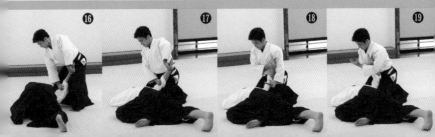

⓰   ⓱   ⓲   ⓳

Ushiro-ryotekubi-dori Dai-sankyo Ura

❶ *Tori* stands face to face with *uke*.

❷ ～ ❹ *Uke* brings *tori*'s knife hand down and moves around to his/her rear. When *tori* brings his/her back foot forward, *uke* grabs *tori*'s both wrists.

❺ ～ ⓫ *Tori* swings both knife hands upward in a spiral motion, brings his/her front foot backward to bring both knife hands down and grabs the back of *uke*'s hand with the inner hand.

⓬ ～ ⓮ *Tori* takes control of *uke*'s elbow with the other hand and brings *uke* facedown onto the mat in a *tenkan* movement.

⓯ ～ ⓱ *Tori* sits in the *kiza* posture with *uke*'s shoulder between both knees, changes the grip from one hand to the other, and locks *uke*'s shoulder joint.

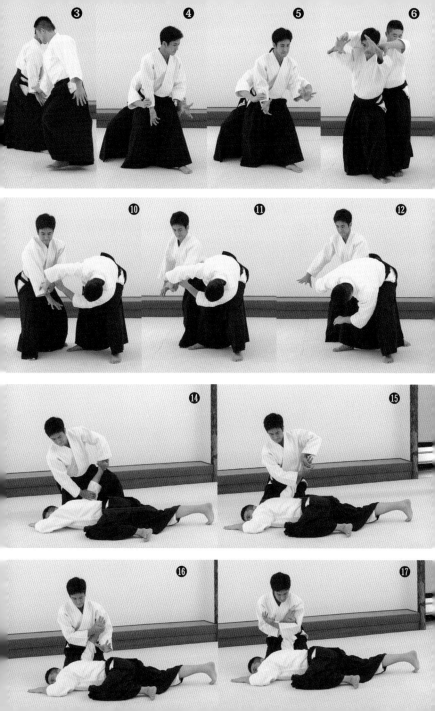

Important Points to Remember in
Ushiro-ryotekubi-dori Dai-sankyo Ura

**The motion in Pictures ❻~❼
seen from a different angle**
Tori brings his/her front foot
backward, swinging both hands
downward, and grabs *uke*'s
hand with the inner hand. *Tori*
then brings his/her front foot into
uke's rear side, takes control of
uke's elbow, and brings *uke*
facedown onto the mat.

❹

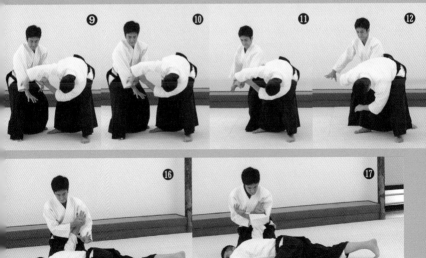

❾ ❿ ⓫ ⓬

⓰ ⓱

❶ ❷

Dai-yonkyo

❻

This is a technique which has wrist-wringing movements—at the inside of *uke*'s wrist in its front variation and the radius (the bone in the forearm on the side of the thumb) in its back variation—in addition to *dai-ikkyo*.

Shomen-uchi Dai-yonkyo Omote

❶ *Tori* stands face to face with *uke*.

❷ ~ ❸ The instant *uke* brings his/her front foot forward and raises his/her knife hand, *tori* brings his/her front foot aside and takes control of *uke*'s elbow and knife hand.

❹ ~❺ *Tori* brings his/her back foot forward to swing *uke*'s arm down.

❻ ~❾ *Tori* takes control of the back of *uke*'s wrist with the hand that has been put on *uke*'s elbow, steps forward to swing *uke*'s arm down, and brings *uke* facedown onto the mat.

❿ *Tori* places his/her weight on the base of his/her forefinger, twisting the hand inward, and wrings the back of *uke*'s wrist.

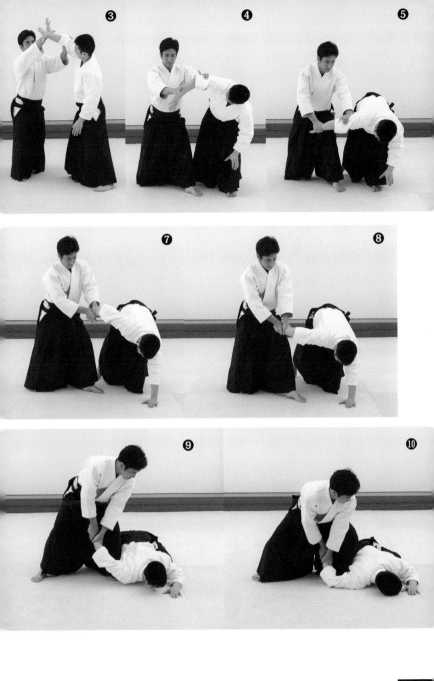

Important Points to Remember in *Shomen-uchi Dai-yonkyo Omote*

The close-up of the motion in Pictures ❻～❿

❻～❾ *Tori* takes control of the back of *uke*'s wrist with the hand that has been put on *uke*'s elbow, steps forward to swing *uke*'s arm down, and brings *uke* facedown onto the mat.

❿ *Tori* places his/her weight on the base of his/her forefinger, twisting the hand inward, and wrings the back of *uke*'s wrist.

The close-up of *tori*'s hands in Picture ❿

Shomen-uchi Dai-yonkyo Ura

❶ *Tori* stands face to face with *uke*.

❷ ~ ❸ The instant *uke* brings his/her front foot forward and raises his/her knife hand, *tori* brings his/her back foot into *uke*'s rear side in an *irimi* movement and takes control of *uke*'s elbow and knife hand.

❹ ~ ❼ *Tori* swings *uke*'s arm down in a *tenkan* movement.

❽ ~ ❿ *Tori* takes control of *uke*'s radius (the bone in the forearm on the side of the thumb) with the hand that has been put on *uke*'s elbow, swings *uke*'s arm down, and brings *uke* facedown onto the mat.

⓫ ~ ⓬ *Tori* places his/her weight on his/her hands and wrings *uke*'s radius with the base of his/her forefinger.

Important Points to Remember in *Shomen-uchi Dai-yonkyo Ura*

The motion in Pictures ⑪～⑫ seen from a different angle
Tori places his/her weight on his/her hands and wrings *uke*'s radius with the base of his/her forefinger.

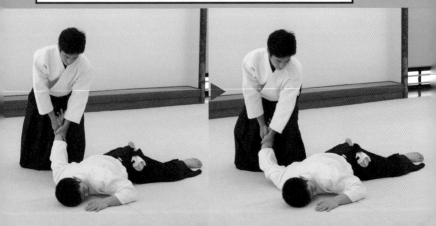

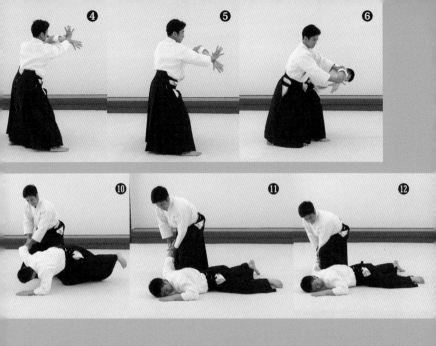

The close-up of *tori*'s hands in Picture ⑩

Developing
Kokyu-ryoku

Kokyu-ho

In aikido, the word *kokyu-ryoku* refers to the power that is effectively exerted from your whole body. *Kyokyu-ho* refers to the method for developing *kokyu-ryoku*, which is mainly transmitted through your knife hand, in sitting and standing positions.

Kokyu-ho Zaho

❶ *Tori* sits face to face with *uke*.

❷～❸ *Tori* lets *uke* grab his/her both wrists with both hands.

❹ *Tori* swings both knife hands upward in a spiral motion.

❺ ～❽ *Tori* moves one of his/her knees slightly forward in the direction where he/she tries to bring *uke* into an off-balance position.

❾ *Tori* brings *uke* faceup onto the mat and pins him/her with both knife hands with the inner knee pressed on *uke*'s side and the outer knee below the wrist.

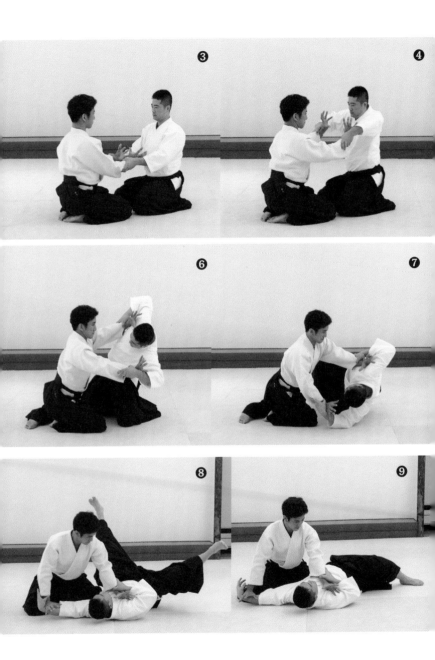

Important Points to Remember in *Kokyu-ho Zaho*

The motion in Pictures ❸〜❽ seen from a different angle

Tori swings his/her hands upward, taking care that his/her elbows do not go outside, and brings the hands from below in a spiral and circular motion. *Tori* then moves one of his/her knees slightly forward in the direction where he/she tries to bring *uke* into an off-balance position.

Tori does not pin *uke* down just with both arms but tries to transmit the force of his/her whole body through both knife hands to *uke*.

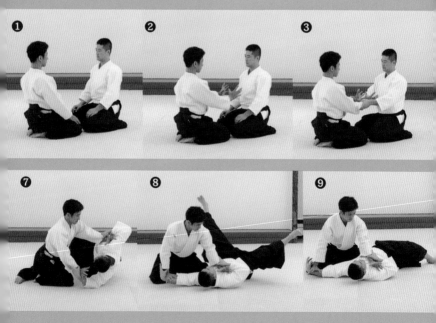

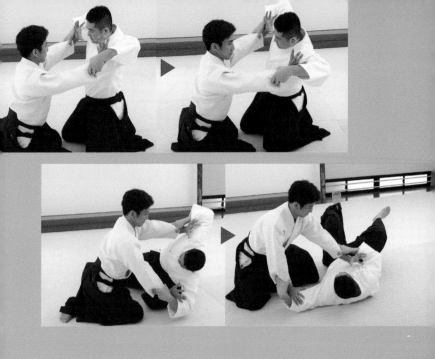

❹ **❺** **❻**

The motion in Picture ❾ seen from a different angle
Tori presses the inner knee on *uke*'s side and the outer knee below the wrist.

Kokyu-ho Rippo
(Morote-dori Kokyu-ho Omote)

❶ *Tori* stands face to face with *uke*.

❷ ~ ❺ *Tori* and *uke* put their knife hands together. *Uke* then takes a *gyaku-hanmi* stance, bringing *tori*'s hand down, and grabs the hand sideways with both hands.

❻ ~ ❽ *Tori* brings his/her back foot forward, raising his/her knife hand from the centre of his/her body.

❾ ~ ⓭ *Tori* takes another step deeper into *uke*'s rear side and swings both knife hands down, twisting his/her waist, to bring *uke* down onto the mat.

The close-up of the motion in Pictures ❹ ～ ❿ seen from a different angle

Tori raises his/her knife hand on the centre line of his/her body. *Tori* then takes another step deeper into *uke*'s rear side and swings both knife hands down, twisting his/her waist, to bring *uke* down onto the mat. It is important to synchronize the movements of upper and lower bodies.

Important Points to Remember in *Kokyu-ho Rippo* (*Morote-dori Kokyu-ho Omote*)

Kokyu-ho Rippo
(*Morote-dori Kokyu-ho Ura*)

❶ *Tori* stands face to face with *uke*.

❷〜❸ *Tori* and *uke* put their knife hands together. *Uke* then takes a *gyaku-hanmi* stance, bringing *tori*'s hand down, and grabs the hand sideways with both hands.

❹〜❾ *Tori* brings his/her front foot into *uke*'s rear side and raises his/her knife hand in a *tenkan* movement.

❿〜⓭ *Tori* brings his/her front foot backward and swings both knife hands down, twisting his/her waist, to bring *uke* down onto the mat.

Important Points to Remember in *Kokyu-ho Rippo* (*Morote-dori Kokyu-ho Ura*)

The motion in Pictures ❸～⓬ seen from a different angle
Tori brings his/her front foot into *uke*'s rear side and raises his/her knife hand in a spiral and circular motion in a *tenkan* movement. *Tori* then brings his/her front foot backward and swings both knife hands down, twisting his/her waist, to bring *uke* down onto the mat.

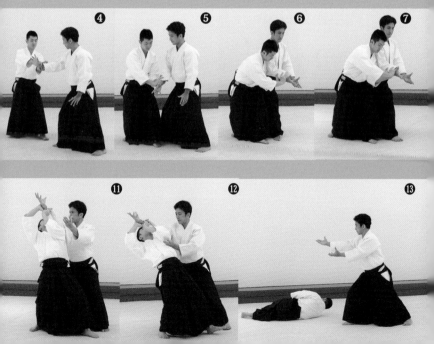

Every year around ten thousand people join All Japan Aikido
Demonstration held at the Nippon Budokan.

Aikido and the Aikikai Public Utility Foundation

What is Aikido?

Aikido is a modern martial art which Master Morihei Ueshiba (1883-
1969), the Founder of Aikido, created after mastering the essence
of traditional martial arts in Japan and further going through hard
mental training.

In aikido, trainees do not compete with each other for the sake of
competition of power. They keep training with each other, through
practicing techniques which are created by such bodily movements as
irimi and *tenkan*, and thereby try to develop themselves mentally and
physically.

Young aikido students from all over Japan join All Japan Training Meeting for Boys and Girls.

Aikido, strongly disapproving of the idea of competition, has no contest at all. It consistently encourages people to respect each other and, for that very reason, is to be considered as one of the best modern martial arts in the present age where harmony among people is strongly needed.

Characteristics of Aikido

Aikido has no contest. It aims to encourage trainees to develop themselves mentally and physically by practicing techniques repeatedly based on their skills and experiences and therefore can be practiced by anybody

Repetition of training not only promotes health, to be sure, but also naturally makes trainees confident enough to positively tackle anything that occurs in their daily lives.

Dojo, where many people differing in age, sex, profession, and nationality get together, provides trainees with good opportunities to

Aikido enthusiasts from all over the world get together in the International Aikido Meeting which is held every four years.

deepen their understanding of human relationships.

Aikido training has no ending. Once you started training, it is advisable to keep on with it strenuously. Pursue the art assiduously. Keeping on with training itself is the first step towards your development and one of the most important aspects of aikido.

Globalization of Aikido

Aikido is popular not only in Japan but also in many parts of the world. Promotion of aikido in foreign countries began in the 1905s, and aikido is now practiced in 140 countries and regions in the world.

The reason why aikido has spread in the world for such a short period of time will be that it has been acknowledged beyond the racial and national borders as an excellent way of mental and physical training.

As a result of the overseas promotion of aikido, the International Aikido Federation (IAF) was founded in 1976, and its general meeting

第12回 国際合気道大会
12th International Aikido Congress

During the International Aikido Congress the representatives discuss the elections of organizers of training sessions, new executives of the Congress, and new member nations, as well as those issues including revision of regulations.

is held every four years. Furthermore, in 1984 the IAF joined the General Association of International Sports Federation (GAISF), which is an international organization of sports, as a regular member.

In recent years, so many active projects for promoting aikido in foreign countries are being carried out not only by Aikikai but also by other organizations including local associations in many countries, the Japan Foundation, and the Japan International Cooperation Agency (JICA) which delegate many aikido instructors. Aikido is now internationally expected to be one of the most precious modern-day cultural assets in the 21st century.

The Aikikai Public Utility Foundation

Aikikai obtained sanction by the government as a nonprofit foundation in 1940 (the 15th year of the Showa era) and has been active as an

National Student Aikido
Demonstration Meeting
for Students

National High School Aikido
Demonstration Meeting

organization that promotes and develops aikido in such a way, as its Founder Morihei Ueshiba intended, that it should benefit society by producing healthy citizens by means of mental and physical training. Its status changed to a public utility foundation on April 1 in the 24th year of the Heisei era.

Activities

· Training at the Hombu Dojo, establishment and operation of Aikido schools, and publication of books and Aikido Bulletins (in Japanese and English)

· Establishment and operation of affiliated dojos, and dispatching of Hombu-Dojo instructors to domestic and foreign countries and regions

· Organization of public demonstration meetings and workshops

· Other activities for promoting aikido

Other organizations that promote and develop aikido:

· International Aikido Federation (IAF; established in 1976)

· All-Japan Aikido Federation (established in 1976)

· Ministry of Defense Aikido Federation (established in 1961)

· National Student Aikido Fedration (established in 1961)

· National High School Aikido Federation (established in 2002)

One of the annual over-year training sessions at the Hombu Dojo

The present Hombu Dojo of Aikido

The Hombu Dojo of Aikido

Morihei Ueshiba, the Founder, moved to Tokyo in 1927 (the second year of the Showa era) and started training, moving from one temporary rented dojo to another, but gradually found it difficult to keep on training at a small dojo as the number of incoming trainees increased. He then founded, with the help of some people including Isamu Takeshita, Admiral of the Japanese Navy, a wooden eighty-mat aikido dojo in the site which is now in Wakamatsu-cho in the Shinjuku ward. The dojo, then called 'Kobukan', is the predecessor of our Hombu Dojo of Aikido.

The Hombu Dojo fortunately escaped air-raid damage during the Pacific War and changed its name, when the Aikikai Foundation was established, to the Hombu Dojo of Aikido, Aikikai Foundation. Training continued even during the period of postwar confusion, and there was a slow but steady increase of members.

In 1967 (the 43rd year of the Showa era) the wooden dojo was remodelled into a three-storied building of reinforced concrete functioning as a modern dojo. Furthermore, in 1973 (the 48th year of the Showa era), the building was extended upward to have the fourth and fifth floors, and the total space of our three training halls currently amount to 250 mats. These three training halls are now fully occupied every day by trainees, who amount to 500 a day.

Brief Personal Records of Successive Doshus

Aikido is a martial art created by Morihei Ueshiba, the Founder. After his death, the position of Doshu [Leader] was succeeded by Kisshomaru Ueshiba, followed by Moriteru Ueshiba, the incumbent Doshu.

Morihei Ueshiba (1883-1969)

1883 Born in Nishinotani Village, Nishimuro County, Wakayama Prefecture (now Uenoyama, Tanabe City, Wakayama Prefecture) on December the 14th.

1908 Got a license of jujutsu of the Yagyu-shingan school from Masanosuke Tsuboi.

1911 Responded to the government's policy of inviting cultivating groups to Hokkaido and migrated the next year to Shirataki-genya, Monbetsu County, Hokkaido, as the leader of the group of developers consisting of fifty-four families. Received instruction in jujutsu of the Daito school from Sokaku Takeda.

1919 Received the news of his father becoming critically ill and left for his home. Made a stopover at Ayabe-cho, Kyoto Prefecture, on the way and met Onisaburo Deguchi of the religious sect of Oomoto and was fascinated by him. Moved to Ayabe, Kyoto with his family after his father's death and established a training dojo called 'Ueshiba Juku'.

1926 Founded a new type of budo, which he called 'Aiki-no-michi [the Way of Aiki]'.

1927 Moved to Tokyo with his family and gave martial instruction at many institutes including the Naval Academy.

1931 Established a dojo specializing in aikido training in Ushigomewakamatsu-cho (now Wakamatsu-cho in the Shinjuku ward).

1940 Had the dojo authorized to become a juridical foundation.

1941 Established an out-door dojo in Iwama-cho, Ibaraki Prefecture.

1955 Devoted himself to the promotion of aikido inside and outside Japan.

1960 Received a Purple Ribbon Medal for his achievement of founding aikido.

1964 Was decorated the Fourth Order of the Rizing Sun, Gold Rays with Rosette.

1969 Died on April the 26th at the age of eighty-six and was conferred the Third Order of the Sacred Treasure (Senior Grade of the Fifth Court Rank) in honour of his achievements in founding and promoting aikido.

Kisshomaru Ueshiba (1921-1999)

1921 Born on June 27th as the third son of Morihei Ueshiba, the Founder of aikido.

1946 Graduated from the School of Political Science and Economics, Waseda University.

1948 Became the Director of the Hombu Dojo of Aikido in place of the Founder.

1967 Took office as the Chief Director of the Aikikai Foundation.

1969 Succeeded to the position of Doshu owing to the Founder's death.

1986 Was conferred a Blue Ribbon Medal for his achievements in promoting aikido.

1995 Was conferred the Third Order of the Sacred Treasure.

1996 Filled many important posts including the President of the International Aikido Federation, President of the Japan Students' Association of Aikido, and Director of the Nippon Budokan Foundation.

1999 Died on January 4th and was conferred the Senior Grade of the Fifth Court Rank by the Japanese government.

Moriteru Ueshiba (1951-)

1951 Born on April 2nd as the second son of Kisshomaru Ueshiba the second Doshu of aikido.

1976 Graduated from the Faculty of Economics, Meiji Gakuin University.

1985 Took office as Managing Director.

1986 Took office as Director of the Hombu Dojo of Aikido.

1996 Took office as Chief Director of the Aikikai Federation.

1999 Succeeded to the position of Doshu owing to the second Doshu's death.

2004 Took office as special lecturer at Tohoku University.

2006 Received an Anchieta Medal of Brazil. Became emeritus visiting professor at International Budo University.

2009 Was awarded the Order of Friendship from the Russian Federation.

2010 Took office as special invited professor at Kogakkan University (till 2017).

2012 Took office as Chief Director of the Aikikai Public Utility Foundation owing to the change of status of Aikikai from an incorporated foundation to public utility foundation.Received the Gold Medal from University of Valencia.

2013 Was conferred a Blue Ribbon Medal for his achievements of publicizing and promoting aikido. Filled many important posts including the Director of the Nippon Budokan Public Utility Foundation and Senator at International Budo University.

About the author:

Mitsuteru Ueshiba was born on June the 27th, 1981 (the 56th year of the Showa era) as a grandson of Morihei Ueshiba, the Founder of Aikido, and the eldest son of Moriteru Ueshiba, the incumbent Doshu of Aikido. After graduating from Toyo University in March, 2006 (the 18th year of the Heisei era) he started working for the Aikikai Foundation and in 2015 (the 27th year of the Heisei era) became the Director of the Hombu Dojo of Aikido. He is currently the Director of Hombu Dojo, the Aikikai (Public Utility) Foundation, which is the very centre of aikido practiced in 140 countries and regions in the world, and is enthusiastically working based in the Hombu Dojo of Aikido for the promotion of aikido in Japan as well as in many parts of the world.

翻訳　斎藤兆史
装幀　ゴトウアキヒロ

An Introduction to Aikido
Mastering the Basics Through Proper Training

英訳版　合気道入門　正確な稽古で基本を極める

発行日	2020 年 3 月 10 日　第 1 刷
著　者	植芝充央
発行者	清田名人
発行所	株式会社内外出版社
	〒 110-8578 東京都台東区東上野 2-1-11
	電話　03-5830-0368　（企画販売局）
	電話　03-5830-0237　（編集部）
	https://www.naigai-p.co.jp
印刷・製本	中央精版印刷株式会社

ISBN 978-4-86257-513-5 C0075

Aikido, the Contemporary Martial Art of Harmony:
Training Methods and Spiritual Teachings

Moriteru Ueshiba
Doshu of Aikido

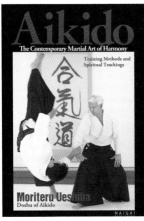

1,600yen
ISBN 9784862573490

Aikido, the Contemporary Martial Art of Harmony: Training Methods and Spiritual Teachings is an introductory book on aikido, which is now enthusiastically practiced at 2,400 dojos in Japan and in 140 countries and regions in the world. Moriteru Ueshiba, the author and Doshu [leader of the head family] of aikido, explains in easy-to-understand words the philosophy, techniques, and training methods of aikido which are designed to enable its trainees to transcend contests and conflicts and to develop themselves mentally and physically in perfect harmony with each other in training. The reader, even without any knowledge or substantial experience of aikido training, will understand what this wonderful martial art is all about.

●e-book
amazon.com
https://www.amazon.com/gp/product/B07ZJ63G5P
●Paper back Overseas shipping/Service in English
Amazon.co.jp
https://www.amazon.co.jp/dp/4862574726

※ Also sold at Kobo and Apple Store.